# HOW AND WHERE TO INVEST YOUR TALENT

JACOB OPOKU

authorHOUSE®

*AuthorHouse™ UK*
*1663 Liberty Drive*
*Bloomington, IN 47403 USA*
*www.authorhouse.co.uk*
*Phone: UK TFN: 0800 0148641 (Toll Free inside the UK)*
*UK Local: 02036 956322 (+44 20 3695 6322 from outside the UK)*

*Published by AuthorHouse 09/17/2020*

*ISBN: 978-1-7283-7918-0 (sc)*
*ISBN: 978-1-7283-7917-3 (hc)*
*ISBN: 978-1-6655-8035-9 (e)*

*Print information available on the last page.*

*Any people depicted in stock imagery provided by Getty Images are models, and such images are being used for illustrative purposes only. Certain stock imagery © Getty Images.*

*This book is printed on acid-free paper.*

*Because of the dynamic nature of the Internet, any web addresses or links contained in this book may have changed since publication and may no longer be valid. The views expressed in this work are solely those of the author and do not necessarily reflect the views of the publisher, and the publisher hereby disclaims any responsibility for them.*

*Scripture quotations marked KJV are from the Holy Bible, King James Version (Authorized Version). First published in 1611. Quoted from the KJV Classic Reference Bible, Copyright © 1983 by The Zondervan Corporation.*

For who maketh thee to differ from another? and what hast thou that thou didst not receive? now if thou didst receive it, why dost thou glory, as if thou hadst not received it?

—1 Corinthians 4:7 (KJV)

All glory and honour goes to God, the giver of life and talents. I am nothing without God. All that I am and all that I will be is God. I cannot thank God enough.

My sincere thanks also go to my wife, Rita. She is the best thing that God has blessed me with, together with our three children, Nana, Lady, and Oheneba. My family inspires and supports me in everything I embark upon.

For all those looking to find and manifest themselves, my sincere prayers are that as you read this book, may God help you to know what your work on earth is. I encourage you to add faith into your success path.

# CONTENTS

# INTRODUCTION

It is surprising that three people are given some resources to work with and two of these people go to work immediately with what they are given. Their hard work pays off, and each of these two people double what was handed to them when accounts were rendered.

Unfortunately, the third person decides to bury what is given him or her, doing nothing with the resource given. When the time comes for accountability, this person returns the resource just the way it was given.

The master or the giver of the resource, after his return and accountability with the first two servants, becomes delightful in their work. The two servants are equally commended, promoted, and given more to manage responsibly.

Meanwhile, the third servant gets into the bad books of the master. He is reprimanded and demoted, and what he had previously is taken away from him.

The story of the third servant is the story of most of us. The Creator has given us talents, knowledge, ideas, visions, dreams, and gifts according to our abilities and capabilities. Unfortunately, some of us concern ourselves so much with other people's talents that we forget we have also been given some talents as well. Some of us wish we had the same talents as others, but He who gives the talents gives them according to our abilities. You have been given an idea which you can manage responsibly.

This book is about who an entrepreneur is and how it all starts. If some people can be successful with their gifts and talents, we can also.

It will take imagination and ideas. Looking into yourself and manifesting that which God has placed in you will be the starting point. God has given you what you can do. It is worth more than you can imagine. When God wanted to create tables, He placed them in trees in the form of wood. God wants you to work and care for the earth that He has beautifully created. By working and cultivating the talents and ideas God has placed in you, you become partners with God in the creation, work, and care of His earth.

Let nothing stand in your way of doubling the talent the master has given you. With no excuse whatsoever and with faith, know that things will work out for your good when you have purpose in your heart and work hard to double the talents God has given you.

# CHAPTER 1

# WHO IS AN ENTREPRENEUR?

With the advent of social media, many people call themselves entrepreneurs. In this chapter, we want to look at what the word *entrepreneur* means so you can appreciate what entrepreneurship is all about. In simple terms, an entrepreneur is someone who has an idea, a vision, or a dream about something that does not exist or an improvement to something that is already in existence.

An entrepreneur is not just a dreamer but is one who works to create a product or service out of the dream he or she has been given, hoping that people will acquire and use it to improve their standards of living. An entrepreneur does this by building a business venture or model to support the sales of the product or service that his or her dreams have produced.

There are three things to remember at this point. First, an entrepreneur receives an idea and has a vision or a dream about a product or service that is non-existent or an improved or modified version of an existing service or product.

Second, an entrepreneur works to turn the dreams, visions, and ideas given to him or her into reality in the form of tangible objects or products and services.

Third, an entrepreneur works to develop means by which the products and services created through her or his dreams can be produced and distributed for a profit to customers who need those products and services to improve their standards of living. The big question is, can anyone become an entrepreneur?

## The Parable of the Talents

> For the kingdom of heaven is as a man travelling into a far country, who called his own servants, and delivered unto them his goods.
>
> And unto one he gave five talents, to another two, and to another one; to every man according to his several ability; and straightway took his journey
>
> —Matthew 25:14–15 (KJV)

From the passage in the Bible above, the answer is clearly yes. According to this passage, when the rich man was going away, he gave money or talent to all three of his servants according to their individual abilities. He did not leave anyone out. But we must appreciate that he did not give them all equal talents. This was not to discriminate or to be biased. The Bible says the rich man gave out the talents according to the servants' abilities.

Another insight we can get from this is that

inspirations, dreams, visions, and ideas differ from one person to another. What inspires and motivates you may be completely different from the other person. This is where originality comes in. Your vision and dreams given to you are different from any other person; therefore, do not copy any other person. Be yourself. The giver of talents, dreams, visions, and ideas knows you and your capabilities better than any other. Follow your dreams and your calling.

The Bible says that the rich man then went away. The rich man knew what the servants could all do. He gave them time to develop and increase what he had given the servants.

One of the greatest and most precious gifts God gave to us humans is the gift of time. Patiently develop your talents and visions given you but also remember that you have no eternity. The name of this talent game is *results*. And when the giver comes back, he will require a result from the gifts given you.

Now back to you. You may be asking yourself what

this story has to do with you. Everything! Let me take you back to the first book of the Bible. It says that God created this wonderful and beautifully good world with all its trees, animals, seas, the sky, and birds. Such beauty of a creation to behold was the earth that God created. Then God created humanity and put them in charge of His beautiful creation to *work* and *care* for it. Does this passage in the Bible mean anything to you regarding your purpose in life?

All humans are the offspring of the first man, Adam, and the first woman, Eve, and we have the same agenda given to Adam and Eve—to work and care for the world we have been brought into. Everyone born has a duty and a purpose to work and care for the earth.

In fact, to work is godly because God first started working. The Bible says that God was busy working for six days and only rested on the seventh day, when all that He planned to do was completed.

When God looked back at the fruit of His labour, He called it 'very good'. God examined and assessed the quality of His work, and when He determined that He had done a good job, God was pleased.

This should tell us that when we work and care for the earth in the highest quality way, the reward for such work is the honour and satisfaction that comes from a job well done.

Another thing to observe is that the Bible says God created Adam and Eve in His image. This could mean image insofar as characteristics. Remember that God is the primary worker and He created us to continue the work He had started with in His world.

The charge to Adam and Eve, hence humanity, was to work, cultivate, bring into fullness or manifest, to foster growth, to improve, and to maintain and care for what God created. Humanity is to preserve from decay, from failure and decline, and protect the things God has already created.

In addition, humanity is to subdue, to exercise control, and to discipline, rule over, administer, and take responsibility for the decisions of our lives and of life. As a person, your work is to find and manifest yourself. You should use your full potential to grow and improve in all aspects of your life.

What I want you to be aware of is that we all have been created to be here among the living because God has a purpose and a work for us to do. You have a work to do, and I have a work to do as well.

Another character trait we learned from God as the first entrepreneur is His innovation, daring nature, and problem-solving techniques. To emulate God, we need a spirit that is characterized by innovation and risk-taking. Be observant and be a problem-solver.

God had the great idea of creating a world as beautiful as ours. He decided to create a man in His image to oversee that beautiful creation. That was so risky, but God went for it. When God started implementing His ideas, He encountered many challenges, but He solved them all. The earth was without form, and darkness covered everywhere. God solved this problem before starting His masterpiece design and creation of the world.

Entrepreneurs from times past have been, now and in the future, an essential part of every society's ability to succeed in an ever-changing and increasingly competitive global marketplace.

## Examples of Entrepreneurs

Bill Gates: He was the co-founder of Microsoft, from the basic idea for computers. Now 90 per cent of the world's computers use Microsoft.

Sam Walton: He was the founder of Walmart and Sam's Club. His simple dream turned into reality.

Ted Turner: He was the founder of CNN.

Henry Ford: He was the president of Ford Motor Company.

Ray Kroc: He was the founder of McDonald's franchising.

Fred Smith: He was the FedEx founder.

Those are a lot of success stories, but wait—there's more. For me, one of the key elements to make the world's economy even better is having the right entrepreneurial mindset. We should take advantage of all the opportunities that come our way.

Today several men from Africa are creating impact in their own fields across the globe. Men such as Aliko Dangote, Strive Masiyiwa, Tony Elumelu, and Elon Musk are some of those entrepreneurial leaders.

## Back to Basics

In our society, if you can turn your ideas into reality, it's one of the solid foundations to an economic success. A world dominated by competitive big business brings bigger responsibilities for our future entrepreneurs.

Different types of moneymaking systems:

- Capitalism
- Traditional system
- Command system
- Mixed economic system

*Capitalism* is an economic system that allows private ownership to earn profits from the goods and services they offer, providing full control and freedom to choose which goods or services to produce and offer, how to produce them, and how much they cost.

Other forms of capitalism:

➢ State owned

➢ Commercial

➢ Community market

An old-fashioned or traditional economy is a structure where traditions, customs, and beliefs shape the goods and products and which services the economy produces, usually used in pastoral-, rural-, and farm-based societies, defined as trading or bartering to exchange goods and services. Even in our modern world, there are still some countries that practice this type of traditional economic system. Hunting and gathering, in addition to cultivation, are the main tasks of workers. Little surplus is produced, and if any extra goods are made, they must be given to the landowner.

The *command economy* is a structure where the

government retains full control and power over the companies that manufactured or produced industrial goods within the country.

A *mixed economy* is a structure where the free market and other economic systems are operated by the government. The government imposes laws and regulation to certain private sectors, which involves delivering services to public, health, education, and waste management.

In capitalism, entrepreneurs do well because they are responsible for such economic decisions as to what to produce, how much to produce, and what methods of production to use.

## The Agricultural Revolution and Entrepreneurship

The agricultural transformation—or revolution, as we call it—was the start of shift in entrepreneurship. People started to control plants and animals. Before long, people had to go widely about in search of food and meat. With time, instead of roaming about in search of food and hunting for animals in different parts of the land, society decided to remain in one location and farm the land for food and rear animals for meat.

This was an important change in human history. The agricultural revolution, or transformation, also meant that there was no longer a need for everyone to be wholly engaged with food cultivation and animal production. There was no longer the need for people to go hunting and gathering to support their families. The agricultural revolution brought about specialization, meaning that a number (not all) of the community members became farmers who handled food production while the rest of the community members focused on other various tasks of the needs of the community.

Specialization introduced different professions; hence, members of the community could exchange valuable goods and services for food. Farmers were then growing more food than they needed to support their own families. They would sell surplus food at the market to, for example, cattle rearers, or cloth makers. The food producer's family no longer needed to make their own clothes or worry about meat. They could rely on the dedicated services of others within the community to provide for their other needs apart from food production. Talents and tricks of a chosen vocation would be handed down through families.

Creativity and young talents increased the pace of innovation. The progression and pace of these specialists brought about increased advantages for the whole community. As time went on, new areas of specialization began to appear.

The extent of wealth and material comfort offered to the people of the community continued to increase. Entrepreneurs were constantly at the lead of innovation. If a problem needed to be solved, these early entrepreneurs admitted that they could profit by solving that problem and therefore moved to take advantage of the problem.

A crucial advancement in the history of entrepreneurship and in human history was the introduction of money. Before the introduction of money, all trade took place through the barter system. For example, if someone named Kwame wanted five tubers of yam, then he might have to trade in seven tubers of cassava to get those yams he desired. One challenge was that, of course Kwame would also need to find a cassava merchant who needed a yam.

'Coincidence of wants', as it was called, limited trade in the early history of humankind. The game changer was the invention of currency. Over time, paper money and coinage were developed.

## The Industrial Revolution and Entrepreneurship

The Industrial Revolution brought about yet another profound shift in the history of entrepreneurship. Entrepreneurship moved from small-scale production in small towns to large-scale production in big cities.

Before this age, due to energy and labour constraints, businesses were limited in how much they could produce. But with the breakthrough in technology and huge population growth, entrepreneurs took advantage of the breakthroughs. Firms were no longer limited by small-scale energy powered by wind (which was weather dependent) or falling water (which was location dependent). Instead, they could rely on technologies like electricity, steam, the internal combustion engine, the locomotive, the automobile, and oil to make large-scale factories.

## Modern Entrepreneurship

Entrepreneurs are the lifeblood of economies all over the world. The global economy means that no longer are entrepreneurs in a location or tribe competing with entrepreneurs in that tribe, town, village, or city alone. Rather, entrepreneurs are competing with entrepreneurs all over the world.

Many of these entrepreneurs can get lower means of production than others can. They may have better access to raw resources and cheap labour. This has made modern entrepreneurship more challenging and at the same time, interestingly, more rewarding than ever before.

# CHAPTER 2

# IT ALL STARTS WITH IMAGINATION

*Einstein claimed that imagination is more
important than knowledge.*

We are affected by our dreams and our visions of the
future. Your imagination about the future determines
how you live your life. Your imagination affects the way
you dress, the food you eat, where you shop and dine, the
courses you pick at school, and the people you choose as
friends and eventually spouses, who your associates are,
and the number of children you decide to have. This also

includes the organization you work with and what and who takes much of your precious time. How you imagine your future affects everything.

Imagination is a tool that gives you unlimited access and freedom to see what is possible for you and the world. Imagination breaks all barriers. Imagination is everything. The beautiful thing is that this great gift and inspiration called imagination from God to the human has no limits and is free.

In the beginning, as I read somewhere in the Bible, there was no earth or universe. God created the heavens and the earth. God created something out of nothing. How did God do all this?

It all started with imagination and ideas. To turn nothing into something, you need ideas and imagination. The Bible says in the beginning that the heaven and earth was not in existence. I believe God did not start to create the earth without having any ideas and imagination about the earth.

I believe God had some ideas and imagination about

the earth and therefore decided to bring His imagination and ideas into reality by creating the heavens and the earth.

In this chapter, we want to learn about idea generation, which is the beginning of entrepreneurship.

Idea development is the state or action of forming new ideas, images, or concepts of external objects that are not present to the senses .This is no other words what is normally called imagination. The process includes constructing through the idea, innovating the concept, developing the process, and bringing the concept to reality.

We shall come back to the ideal development process, but for now let us give our attention to the concept of imagination and ideas.

Imagination is that which permits people to travel mentally and experience things that are not in our present world or may be not even be real. For example, right now as you are reading this book, you may be imagining, daydreaming about your desire, or wishing for mansion(s), car(s), private jet(s), clothing, shoe(s), bag(s), a fat bank balance, family, organization, business, enterprise, holiday trips, job, finance, popularity through your talents and gifts, spouse, and your ministry, to mention but a few.

What is important to note is that what is imagined, wished for, desired, or dreamed is generated from within; God and no one else has given it to you. Dreams are from within rather than something you come to understand or become aware of based on input from without. God inspires it in you; no one else does. That is why your desires and dreams are different from everyone else's. That is why nobody but you alone understands your dreams.

Imagination is the beginning of reality.

—Jim Rohn

So God created man in His own image; in the image of God created he him; male and female created he them.

—Genesis 1:27 (KJV)

And God blessed them, and God said unto them, Be fruitful, and multiply, and replenish the earth, and subdue it: and have dominion over the fish of the sea, and over the fowl of the air, and over every living thing that moveth upon the earth.

—Genesis 1:28 (KJV)

I earlier stated my belief that even the Creator of the universe first had a mental picture of how and what He wanted the universe to be and how it should be taken care of before He started work. Hence, when He had finished all His work, according to the Bible (Genesis 1:31 KJV): 'And God saw everything that He had made, and, behold, it was very good. And the evening and the morning were the sixth day.'

God went back to His original ideas and imagination about the universe, and on comparison with His actual work about the universe, He was very pleased. God had achieved His desire, and the Bible says God saw all that He had created and it was good.

God was happy that His imagination had finally come through after times of planning and execution. If we have been created in the image and likelihood of the Creator, then it means we all can have ideas and imaginations about the realities of what is possible for us. The imagination and ideas of God know no bounds.

Alexander Graham Bell, the inventor of the telephone, imagined a world where he could send messages to people over a long distance on a single wire, and that imagination and ideas gave birth to telephones that we use today.

Martin Cooper said that watching Captain Kirk using his communicator on the television show *Star Trek* inspired him with a stunning idea: to develop a handheld mobile phone. And now mobile phones have become an essential part of our everyday lives.

German engineer Karl Benz imagined a horseless carriage, and that gave birth to car manufacturing, which today gives us privacy and the majority of us cars as a safe and faster means of reaching our destinations.

The Wright brothers imagined a flying machine, and

today airplanes have made this world small, changing travel times from months to hours.

It was the imagination of people like Thomas Edison to see a world where we can lighten a dark space without necessarily daylight from nature, which led to the invention of the electric bulbs. Today electric bulbs are not only used for light but used to show an electronic device is on, to direct traffic, for heat, and for many other purposes. Billions are in use, some even in outer space. The light bulb profoundly changed human existence by illuminating the night and making it hospitable to a wide range of human activity.

Michael Faraday came up with electricity, and today electricity is an essential part of modern life and important to every world economy. People use electricity for lighting, heating, cooling, refrigeration, and for operating appliances, computers, electronics, machinery, and public transportation systems.

Sir Francis Bacon first imagined the idea that cold could be used to preserve meat versus methods from centuries ago, when people gathered ice from streams and ponds and did their best to store it year-round in icehouses and cellars so they had a ready supply to keep their food cold. That idea has been worked on, and today refrigerators have become everyday essential equipment in homes and establishments.

Philo Taylor Farnsworth began to think of a system that could capture moving images, transform those images into code, and then move those images along radio waves to different devices. That was the genesis of electric television.

Mark Zuckerberg imagined a tool platform where people could go and learn about other people, and Facebook is now a large part of history.

Jeff Bezos imagined an online store where you could shop anytime you want, as the shop never closed, and today Amazon.com is considered one of the big four technology companies, along with Google, Apple, and Facebook, with the biggest turnover in 2019, making the CEO, Jeff, the richest man in the world in 2019.

People like Charles Babbage, who is considered the father of the computer, Tim Berners-Lee the internet (World Wide Web) are inventors of people who worked with their imaginations to create the better world that we enjoy today. It is your turn to bring your imagination into reality to change the world for the better.

You will surely agree with me that the successful people we see today have imagined and used the imaginative parts of their minds and asked questions like, 'How else can this challenge be looked at? How else can this concern be dealt with? What other possibilities do I have?'

Even America today, according to the late Ronald Reagan, is a dream: 'The Republic is a dream. If we don't keep dreaming, we will lose the republic.'

You see, my friend, that imagination, desire, dreams, and wishes are everything as far as economic progress is concerned. To make something from nothing and create the world that we wish to see, we need to harness the gift of imagination that God has inspired in us, knowing that *all* things (imaginations and ideas) are possible to those who believe.

Some Tips to Develop Positive Imaginations

## Mind Wandering

When your mind wanders about the reality of possibilities, you are daydreaming. According to a survey, daydreaming isn't necessarily a bad thing. It might be a sign that you're smart and creative. People with efficient brains may have too much brain capacity to stop their minds from wandering.

During daydreaming, you take yourself out of the ordinary moment and open yourself to possibilities. Daydreaming is an exercise that can open your imagination to new ideas and dreams. Those new ideas and dreams can help you thrive in every aspect of your life. After daydreaming, you can return to the situation with a new attitude and possibly even a solution to the concern that you needed to address.

Daydreaming can also raise your mood and give you that feel-good factor. The better you feel, the more likely you are to be productive. For example, if you can daydream of being successful at a task you have set for yourself or become a successful person in life, you are more likely to reach your goals. Visualization is often an important key to reaching your destination, and daydreaming can help you concentrate and focus on a higher goal for yourself. The more you think about your goal and focus on the steps to achieving that goal, the more likely you will be to reach it.

## Reading

Reading can give us imagination, and it inspires us to think of new ideas and strategies. It is said that reading is the best workout for the brain. The brain is the most complex organ and command centre of the whole body. The brain is responsible for so many important functions, so please do not ignore or even take your brain for granted.

Just as we want to exercise our bodies and get in shape, we must also exercise our brains.

Reading is good for your mind, body, and soul. Reading five to ten pages means you are 'waking up' your brain and stimulating the thought process. Make this a daily habit. You can also do this in the evening before you go to sleep. You also have to be mindful with what you feed your mind. Read inspiring books in areas of interest. By so doing, you can transform not only how you see yourself but also how you see the world.

## Writing

I read somewhere in the Bible that God asks people to write what visions and instructions He gives them. That made me realize the importance of writing. There is an old Chinese saying that the faintest ink is more powerful than the strongest memory. I therefore recommend that you carry a pocket-sized journal, a tablet, or a smartphone with you everywhere you go and put down thoughts, ideas, and imagination into this medium of writing.

Find some relaxing place like a cafe, library, or park and just sit and put your imagination into your journal, tablet, or smartphone. The whole idea is to spend quiet moments with yourself and write out your thoughts and imaginations. This creative exercise opens your imagination to new ideas for work and solutions to some of the roadblocks of your life. The truth is that your memory can prove very unreliable when it comes time to recall such brilliant ideas, but a few notes recorded while the imagination is still fresh can prove very helpful. Sounds good, right? So why not find a good pen and some paper, a tablet, or a smartphone and get started writing down your ideas?

## We All Have the Imaginative Tool

Everyone can imagine. There are no special selected people who have the right to imagine. Imagination is simply the ability of the brain to think in pictures of the reality of the possibility in the future. In daydreaming, we imagine just we as we do in planning, remembering, and in meditating. What I want to say is that you can start to imagine what you want your life, your relationship, your home, your marriage, your business, and your finances to be like. You have just as much right as anybody else to imagine and go to work on how you want your life to be. You also have the right to imagine how you want to change the world just as other people have done and brought so much comfort to us through their imaginations.

Earlier I shared my thoughts about how God imagined the earth and eventually breathed life into His imagination with the creation of the world. Somewhere in the Bible, it also says, 'God created mankind in His own image and kind.' This means that this character and image of God (imaginative part) is a gift to all humankind. Through God's creative imagination, He created the universe from nothing. God saw in His mind pictures of the past, the present, and the future. That shows that God himself imagines.

Creative imagination is a gift from God to you, so start meditating, planning, daydreaming, reading, and writing all the imaginations in a journal, smartphone, or on a tablet.

*Remember that nothing you imagination is too crazy or impossible.*

## Future of Entrepreneurship

From the start of history's revolution, the market forces known as supply and demand have always motivated entrepreneurship. Early entrepreneurs in the agricultural revolution met the needs of farmers by providing them with tools and shelter in exchange for food that could feed their families.

The means of entrepreneurship changed as the years went by, but the main motivation for entrepreneurship has remained the same. Around the world, entrepreneurs rise to address a problem/demand by providing a solution/ supply.

Meanwhile, competition has ensured that the entrepreneur's self-interest doesn't cause an overall negative impact on society. For example, competition prevents entrepreneurs from overcharging for goods or underpaying employees.

The human population is ever increasing with its associated demands and ever-increasing standards of living. This means that the entrepreneur is going to be ever needed. Entrepreneurs are and will continue to have a special place in society and be the lifeblood of all economic success around the world.

## CHAPTER 3

# IT IS POSSIBLE

All things are possible to them that believe.

—Annie Rix Militz

In the previous chapter, we finished off with the assurance that it is your right to imagine and think about all the realities that are possible in your mind. It is in your DNA because God gave it to you as a gift. God himself is a creative imaginer, and we are created in His imagine, hence making us creative imaginers as well.

*Believe that what you imagine is possible for you.*

Indeed, all things are possible to those who believe. It is not 'the believing' that does the magic of bringing imaginations into reality but the belief in your imagination that makes you work on your imaginations.

Again going back to the book of Genesis in the Bible, God believed in His imagination and hence went forth to execute His plan, making it a reality in six days. God did not concentrate on the challenges but embraced the beauty and the glorious earth He was about to create.

You may be wondering whether God faced any challenge when He imagined creating the earth. Obviously, *yes*, God also had challenges. Remember, the Bible says the earth was without form. The earth was formless, and darkness was everywhere on the face of the earth. There were two big challenges: a formless earth and darkness all over.

But God could only see the picture of earth in His mind, and as it is said, where there is a will, there is always a way. God went to work, and the creation of the earth is history.

As you maximize your creative imaginative tool, you too can come against some challenges that will want to kill and shut down your dreams. Remember that anything one believes will be tested; therefore, your commitment to your imagination and dreams will also be tested.

## Possible Challenges to Overcome

The first possible challenge is *yourself.* I am referring to all the excuses you give yourself as to why you cannot make your possibility a reality. Why do we give ourselves excuses all the time?

Human nature is to be defensive, to react to anything that interferes with our 'comfortable state'. For example, when the eye sees any chance of danger, it naturally blinks for protection. It is so much so that we act on impulse every day without deliberately giving it a thought, especially when we are in danger of attack.

Our minds will fight anything that will put us out of our comfort zones. For example, when you want to exercise your body and keep fit, it will ache and tell you that it is painful and you should therefore stop.

The body naturally will not want to be put out of its comfort zone.

At its very core, excuses are nothing more than your mind fighting you against its comfort zone. An excuse therefore justifies your self-limiting beliefs.

For us to fight back and move out of our comfort zones, disbelieve our excuses, and begin to pursue our dreams, we need to look at the limiting beliefs underneath and turn them around into a self-belief that's more supporting.

Self-doubt is sometimes unbelievable. So many of us do not believe in our own abilities and skills. For many of us, we don't think good things are meant for us. We think we do not deserve any good things happening to us. We cannot imagine it happening for us. We think good things only happen to some few privileged people. Actually, our excuses are what can stand in the way of our biggest and most audacious dreams.

One of the most common excuses we all have and

hear sometimes for not doing something is *lack of enough time.* The truth is that we can never have enough time. The twenty-four hours in the day will not be increase to thirty or forty-eight hours. It is not how much is given to you but how you utilize what has been given to you that counts. Those who have seen and made their imaginations a reality have and still have the same twenty-four hours in the day that we complain not to be enough.

Some will argue that their schedules are so tight that they have no time to pursue and make their imaginations a reality.

If it really matters to you that you give birth to your dreams and ideas that God has given only to you, you will find a way if that dream is important to you. Remember that where there is a *will*, there is a *way*.

If we examine how we spend our twenty-four hours in a day, we will see that we use that time on things that add less value to our lives than pursuing our dreams and ideas. After all, what's more important: to be on WhatsApp and Facebook, Twitter, and Instagram, flipping and scrolling, reading comments for thirty minutes to one hour or spending thirty minutes researching, finding, and taking one step towards your big dream? If you need more time, look for the little pockets of your life where you can make more time and start from there.

Some people jump into the 'I don't have enough money' excuse. But have you asked yourself or worked out the actual amount of money your dream or ideas will require starting? Exactly what does 'enough' money means in figures? Once you know the exact figure in your mind, you are in a much better position to work towards raising that figure, whether through saving, asking for a bank loan, taking on more work, or selling some of your belongings.

We forget just how many skills we have acquired already in our lifetimes. Running, selling, talking, driving, researching, cooking, typing, editing, saving, and many others are all things that we take for granted—skills that we have spent time learning. That means we as humans can adopt and change to learn new things all the time. The excuse of 'I don't have enough skills' must not be entertained again in your life. Nothing must stop you from taking the time to learn one or two more skills if that will make your dreams come to reality.

If you are telling yourself you are not clever and intelligent enough to do something, you will not be able to do it. If you are finding it difficult to trust your capabilities and skills, take a moment to write down all the things you can do, even the obvious ones: writing, reading, listening, counselling, organizing, washing, cooking, ironing, planning, managing, driving, singing, and dancing.

This is proof that you are capable and have what it takes to realize your dreams and make them a reality. Please give yourself the chance and allow the permission to grow so you can be someone who achieves your dreams.

There are so many other excuses that we give ourselves when it comes to pursuing our dreams: 'I'm not experienced enough, I'm not connected enough, it's too risky, it's too soon, it's too late, it's too unimportant.'

Instead of viewing these excuses as roadblocks, we ought to be asking questions such as what can we do about them?

In case you do not know or have forgotten, you were not born with the skills you have today; you were not born experienced or as well connected as you are today. Everything that you have acquired has been done with the passage of time. The skills, wealth, money, jobs, connections, friends, and experience have all been developed one day at a time. Everyone and everything must start from somewhere at some point in time. The sooner you start, the better for you, so I suggest you start now.

## Do Not Pretend about the Present Challenge

I have to emphasize here that it does not mean we pretend about these challenges. I will go back to the account of the Bible where God created the earth from nothing but His imagination. The account identified the challenges: darkness on the whole earth face and the formless nature of the earth. God did not pretend these challenges were not there but looked for ways to overcome those challenges.

All the challenges and excuses that might put us off might be true, but what I am proposing is that they should not be a reason to give up.

Instead of making identifications of all your excuses stopping you from living your dreams, your attitude should be 'How can I overcome these challenges in order to see my ideas become a reality?' Ask yourself if your idea is a risky one; whether you have to give up your stable job; and what you can do, prepare, or change to minimize the risk?

Whatever excuses are on your mind, make a list as to why you cannot make your dreams a reality. It is important to critically analyse and get to the bottom and specifics behind your excuse.

Reid Hoffman, founder of LinkedIn, famously said,

'If you're not embarrassed by the first version of your product, you've launched too late.'

You will eventually find out that it is 'fear'—**f**orce **e**vidence **a**ppearing **r**eal. We fear that we will fail and embarrass ourselves; we are afraid of stepping out into the unknown; we are afraid of rejection and disapproval of other people.

You are not 'too old', or 'too young', and it will not 'take too long' for you to realize your dreams. Remember that even with God, it took him some time to see his imagination become a reality. It took God six days to perfect His creation of the earth. You might be thinking, *But it took God only six days to create the earth out of nothing.* I remember reading somewhere in the Bible that a thousand years can be one day, and one day for God can be a thousand years. All I am trying to imply is that it took time for God to put the earth together to make it this beautiful and enjoyable.

It is also true that we all have an allocated amount of time on this planet. We do not have all the time like

God has to do all that we want to do. That alone should inform you that time is going to pass whether we are pursuing our dreams or not—so why waste any more time and not do the most we can?

All of us came with a vision and dream. It is therefore very important that you give birth to your dreams. It's your dream, and that's exactly why it is important.

The chances are that you will die with all those books, ideas of better management, business, and enterprises if you do not pursue them and make them a reality. Imagine that the idea of the car died with the first person. Imagine if the idea of the plane, electricity, Internet, social media, computer, and all the great inventions of our times were not pursued what our world would be like. Your ideas are important to you and the rest of the world so start pursuing them now.

My imagination and ideas are such big dreams that they are daunting to start. I guess someone is feeling overwhelmed by the size of the project in front of them. Do not worry. Worry takes a lot of energy out of you. It is very true that where there is a will, there is always a way. Start to look for and seek help. You will be amazed where and how help will come, for it is written, 'For everyone who asks receives: the one who seeks finds and the one who knocks the door will be opened.'

Whatever God has impressed on your heart has not been done before. It could be an improvement on a previous version or an entirely new product or service. Before you write off your dream with an excuse that 'no one has done it so therefore it is impossible', spend a few minutes of your time researching for world record breakers. Before they made those records, no one had done what they did before. You are no different from those people.

This excuse usually has an element of truth to it. 'I have parents, a mortgage, and children to take care of.' Yes, every change of course will affect something. Identify how pursuing your dream might affect your ability to support the other people in your life who need you. For example, pursuing your dream might mean taking a pay cut for a while or moving. Talk to the people concerned, explain how important your dream is, and negotiate with them. Reason with them about ways you can pursue your dream without sacrificing yours or their well-being or happiness.

## Social Pressure from Family and Friends

When you dream big dreams such as becoming the first billionaire in your family, some family and friends will likely jump in to tell you how unlikely that would be. Of course, it is unlikely. That is why it's a big dream.

Have you ever expressed your dream of being somebody or being in a position and noticed some strange looks such as a raised eyebrow or pursed lips? Sometimes it may even be a heavy sigh or a comment such as 'Oh, really?'

This reminds me of a story in the Bible about a lad called Joseph. This young lad had a dream that one day even his father and mother would bow down and worship him.

Upon hearing this big dream, the father of this young lad rebuked him and I guess even told him how unlikely that dream would come to be. His family, especially the elderly siblings, had hatred for him because they could not see it for themselves and therefore would not want to see it for this lad. One event led to another, and the lad was eventually sold into slavery, where with time he rose up to become the prime minister in a foreign land.

This happened without his family knowing anything about the realization of his dreams in a different kingdom. Because of famine in the land where his family lived, his family went to a land where there was plenty of food, and this kingdom happened to be where this young lad had now risen to be the prime minister. To cut a long story short, the whole family, including his father and mother, came there and worshipped him.

Apart from *self*, another killer of imagination and dreams not being made into reality is family and friends. Let me illustrate this further but know that I do not mean to say friends and family are bad. The truth is that your dreams are your dreams and not their dreams. It is you who God impressed upon your heart those imaginations, not theirs. Some of the time, trying to seek family and friends' approval will lead to discouragement and eventually abandonment of your dreams. As a culture, we get so afraid of disappointment. The message is always clear: It's better not to dream big than to be disappointed.

Why? What's so bad about disappointment? If anything, it's character-forming and makes you work harder, and while it may upset you and disillusion you for a while, is it not better than a life lived in fear and avoidance?

There are two types of social dream killers: family and friend groups are those who just cannot see it for themselves and therefore cannot see it for you or anyone else. Such families and friends are so negative that they think they do not deserve anything good happening to them so they cannot see it happening for you. They cannot see themselves as part of the few privileged people who deserve wealth, happiness, success, and abundance so they cannot imagine or accept that you can be among the privileged ones. The fact that nobody has done it successfully in the family and friends circle does not mean you are not qualified or entitled to be a success.

Then we have the second group of family and friends dream killers called 'good intention'. These family and friends kill our dreams not because they want to but rather because they want what's best for us and have more experience. They tend to *think* they know what's best for us and are so scared of disappointment and failures.

The irony is that your parents may be killing your dreams, courtesy of *'only wanting the best for you'*. Your family and friends, of course, tell you what you could do and be what you want but that is better to follow a certain career path; get good grades; go to a good university; and get a good job, spouse, house, kids, and earn $80,000 per year. *Whose dream is this, anyway? Theirs.*

Another big question is why the fear of failure? What is so bad about failures and disappointment? If anything, these two are character forming; they make one work harder. Failure and disappointment may be upsetting for a while, but it is far better than living a life filled with fear and avoidance.

If you have African family and friends, as I proudly do,

you know many of our parents gave us very few options. One must be an engineer, a lawyer, or a medical doctor. Anything less and you are a disgrace to the family. This is because those three fields—engineering, law, and medicine—have proven to be sources of development for the African continent and hence the families. These fields are a secure financial way out, if you will, and a source of pride for the parents.

No wonder many African professionals hate their jobs. Many dreams have been shuttered in the African, Caribbean, and most developing countries because of this second group of family and friends. If you are reading this book and have not yet given up on your dreams, *please* don't. Give your dreams and ideas a shot with all your might and time but please be certain that you are comfortable with the trade-offs and consequences.

I am without any shadow of doubt that as you step into your dreams with faith, God will strengthen you in order for you to accomplish your destiny.

# CHAPTER 4

# SOME INSPIRATIONS

Opportunities don't happen. You create
them.

—Chris Grosser

Hardly any dream or imagination becomes a reality
so easily and effortlessly without delays, problems, or
challenges here or there. It appears as if one must overcome
many obstacles, challenges, and maybe even suffer some
pain before achieving or seeing the manifestation of one's
dreams.

And the bigger your dreams, the tougher your challenge, the more ambitious your goals, the more likely it is that you will face difficulties on your way towards achieving them. When this happens, what will you do?

This chapter is to let you know that you are not alone. Do not just give up. Press on towards the dream and persist against the struggle. Once you have done this, there is only one outcome: *success*.

Whatever struggle, challenge, or excuse is stopping you from your dreams, know that numerous people in history had the same challenges and struggles as you have but with courage pressed on and succeeded. If they could do it, you and I can also do it.

Some great achievers pressed on and prevailed even when everybody and circumstances were yelling at them to quit.

These people did not throw in the towel; therefore, they turned their days of adversity into lifetimes of success.

## Courageous People We Can Learn to Take Inspiration From

### Frederick Douglass, African American social reformer

Frederick Douglas was born on February 1818 in Maryland as Frederick Augustus Washington Bailey. He was best known for his autobiography, *Narrative of the Life of Frederick Douglass, an American Slave.* But how did an American slave become a writer, an American social reformer, an abolitionist, an orator, and a public official given the fact that he was separated from his mother when he was born and lived with his slave master? He grew up with a lack of education, but because of his willingness to learn, he went through self-education. He learned to read and write in secret by observing the writings of his master and the children in the vicinity.

When he started working at the plantation, he began teaching other slaves, but it didn't take long. After escaping from slavery, he started attending abolitions meetings, gaining notes for his oratory and incisive antislavery writings. He believed in the equality of all people. He shared his personal experience as a slave to become a revelation and inspire people. Most interesting!

## Franklin D. Roosevelt

Franklin D. Roosevelt was well known for his initials 'FDR.' Despite his physical challenges, he was one of the greatest US presidents and set a winning record of four successive presidential elections. Yes, he had walking challenges. During his vacation in Canada, he fell ill. He was diagnosed with poliomyelitis at that time. The illness left him permanently paralysed from the waist down. Regardless of his condition, it didn't stop him from achieving his ambitions. When he became a US president, he made sure never to use a wheelchair. Any idea why? As for me, I believe he wanted to show his people that he was a strong and reliable leader. That is the reason why he was wearing iron braces on his legs and hips to walk. Brave!

# Wilma Rudolph

She was an African American woman sprinter born on June 23, 1940. At a very young age, she suffered illness and disability. Yes, a world record–holding Olympic champion had contracted infantile paralysis when she was four years old. Because of that, she had to wear a brace on her left leg. With her huge determination, she was able to overcome it, which led her to achieve her goals.

In the 1956 Summer Olympic Games, she won a bronze medal in the 400-metre relay. In the 1960 Olympics, she won a gold medal in the 100-meter individual. She won a gold medal in the 200-metre individual. She won a gold medal in the 4 x 1 meter relay.

Amazing! In a single Olympics, she won three gold medals. Despite all the things that she had been through, no one could imagine that she would become an international sports icon in track and field.

# Harland David Sanders

An American businessperson, best known as 'Colonel Sanders', he was raised by a single mom because his father died when he was six years old. He needed to take care of his siblings and started working as a farmhand at the age of ten.

In 1903, when he found labouring work at Norfolk and Western Railway, he met his future wife, Josephine King. But sometimes thing happen that can change our lives forever. After the tragic death of his son and loss of his job, his wife left him, along with their children.

Even with all the struggles and problems, he continued to start all over again. He started selling fried chicken at a service station and he was eventually called 'Kentucky Colonel.' However, tragedy struck again, which led to selling his restaurants. Instead of giving up, he used all those failures to motivate himself to move forward. When he was able to borrow money, he used it as capital to continue his fried chicken business from door to door until he opened a new restaurant that was soon called

KFC. The company's growth and international success overwhelmed him, which led him to sell it in 1962 to a group of investors for $2 million.

Life is a bit unfair, don't you think? When we are on the edge of success, problems and tragedy will sometimes pull us down. It's just a matter of how you will look at it. Are you letting it pass you by or moving forward to face and fight it?

## Helen Keller

Helen Adams Keller was born on June 27, 1880. She was an American author, political activist, and lecturer. However, she was also a deaf-blind notable author and humanitarian. Despite her disabilities, she was able to inspire people worldwide.

She was nineteen months old when she suffered from an illness that affected her hearing and vision. Still, it was not enough of a hindrance for her not to become one of the world's most extraordinary women. She wrote books and travelled around the world to give lectures. She also committed her life to improving the conditions of deaf and blind people. If you are a person with a disability, don't lose hope. The world is beautiful, and just like Helen, you can also do things that can change your life or those of people around you.

## Paul Revere Williams

Paul Revere Williams was born on February 18, 1894, in Los Angeles. He was the first black architect to become a member of the American Institute of Architects. How was that possible?

Did you know that his father died when he was just two years old? Then, two years later, his mother passed away. He was an orphan at the age of four and was sent to a foster home.

In his primary school, he was the only African American student. His teacher encouraged him not to pursue architecture because of his colour. Unbelievable! But no one could stop him. He was determined to pursue what he wanted. He believed in his own talent and used it as a stepping stone to gain professional experience in Los Angeles firms. His unique drawing skill led him to design an estimated 2,500 buildings, including the homes of numerous celebrities such as Cary Grant, Lon Chaney, Frank Sinatra, Lucille Ball, and Charles Correll.

## Abraham Lincoln

Abraham Lincoln was born on February 12, 1809, in Kentucky. He was the sixteenth president of the United States and was one of the greatest presidents in the history of the country. His life is an inspiration for all. He was nine years old when his mother passed away. From a very young age, he preferred to spend time reading and writing rather than pursuing physical activities. At the age of twenty-three, he started running his own business.

He started his political career in March of 1832. He won a seat in the state legislature in 1834. In 1846, he won for Congress. In 1860, his determination and perseverance led him to success when he won as the president of the United States.

But did you know that Abraham Lincoln also experienced heartbreak when the love of his life, Ann Rutledge, passed away? It was one of the darkest parts of his life. He suffered nervous breakdowns and numerous political defeats. But it didn't become enough of a hindrance to stop him. He continued to fight and move on.

Let us look at your dream this way. Imagine you are setting out on a romantic getaway holiday trip with your spouse or partner. Everything is prepared and ready for that long-awaited lazy week-long vacation to your dream destination. You get to the airport and learn that your airline company ran into administration issues overnight and all flights are cancelled. The company, however, gives you an option to use a coach to get to the place. The driver then takes you through the journey by words.

It will be a smooth ride from the start ... until halfway along the planned route. The navigation will then take you through a countryside with curvy, narrow, rough, and bumpy road. You will have to drive along an unpaved path with potholes and pits, with bushes and brambles scraping the side of the coach. It's going to be an uncomfortable ride, with a lot of jolting and bumping in your seat. Unfortunately, this is the only way you can get to that lovely romantic location you have paid for and planned for for months.

## What Do You Do?

Remember that your heart was set on this holiday spot. There are quite a lot of decisions you can make. You can change your plans, get a taxi, and go back home. You can also plan and look for another holiday destination if you have money and time. Alternatively, you can curse and swear at the discomfort and take the coach ride with the company to your dream holiday location.

You can count your blessings and be happy about having a coach to get you there even if it's an alternative route, a bad one.

To be honest, if you truly love that location and want to be there at all costs you will even be willing to get down and walk the rest of the way if the coach cannot even drive through.

Hold on a minute. Do you realize that this journey could be your life and the path could be your growth path? The coach is you. The driver is your attitude. If the 'driver', meaning your attitude, is decisive and wants to succeed at all costs, you won't give up. The courage and persistence to keep going on, past hurdles and obstacles, is powered by purpose. Your purpose is a romantic getaway at a secret escape with your loved one. For me, there would be no choice. To give up is to die.

## What Drives You to Keep Going in Your Life?

The answer to that question will lead you towards your powerful purpose. Any endeavour driven and fuelled by purpose cannot fail. *Winners never quit and quitters never win!*

The courage and persistence to keep going on, past hurdles and obstacles, is powered by purpose. Discover it. Tap into it. Achieve it. Ultimately, that's what success means.

These notable successful people we have seen earlier on in this chapter had to deal with numerous challenges. However, they still made it to their eventual goal of accomplishing all that they wanted. Despite their pasts, they still made it towards their success.

The paths of our imaginations may be difficult and tough to deal with, but such is the route to success. Have you ever wondered why many minerals such as like gold and diamonds are buried deep in the ground? Nothing precious is handed to you on a silver platter.

If these famous people could do it, we can do it too.

# CHAPTER 5

# YOU ARE ALREADY A SUCCESS STORY

Your playing small does not serve the world. There is nothing enlightened about shrinking so that other people will not feel insecure around you. We are all meant to shine, as children do. It is not just in some of us; it is in everyone, and as we let our light shine, we unconsciously give others permission to do the same. As we are liberated from our fear, our presence automatically liberates others.

—Marianne Williamson

# Are You a Success Story? If Not, Why?

For me, a story of pregnancy is one of the most amazing stories that I will ever hear. That is why I can't help using it as a best example. Have you ever realized that the moment you were born that alone gives you assurance that you are already a success?

Now, the process of pregnancy may seem simple, but a critical analysis will inform you as to how complicated and timely things must be.

1. Not only must a woman must ovulate a mature egg, but the father must also produce enough strong swimming sperm.
2. The sperm must reach the egg, and the egg must change its structure to become a fertilized embryo.
3. The genetic material of the embryo must be correct; the embryo must divide correctly until it forms a blastocyst; and the blastocyst must implant in the womb without being rejected.

There are so many conditions with getting pregnant that it is no wonder some people experience problems conceiving. Things can easily go wrong.

Have you ever wondered why only you out of all the fourteen million sperms survived and made it to your mother's egg?

I read in the Bible that God says He knew us before we were even formed in our mother's wombs. God knew us before we were born, and He has set us apart. God has appointed us as prophets to nations. A birth is a success story on its own.

Let me ask you this question. When you read about success stories of others, do you ever imagine that others can also be reading about your success story? I think you should ask yourself that question. Seriously. Right now. Why do you perhaps think you are not a success story? Let me give you a minute to think about it. You might take a break at this moment, go for a refreshing beverage, and think about why you have not been a success story. Perhaps some of these thoughts will cross your mind:

a) I have not had the opportunities others had.

b) I have made poor choices in life.

c) I lack the knowledge or experience.

d) I am not motivated or inspired enough.

e) I have no idea; I am reading this to find out.

Did I guess right with any of my above suggestions as to why you think you have not been a success story thus far?

If you chose the first option or something similar, you are essentially saying it is not your fault, that you are a victim. We all play the blame game. When things do not go the way we expect them to, it is very easy to blame everybody and everything but ourselves. We hardly accept responsibilities for what happens to us. We must know that every situation and condition that we find ourselves in was because of our own actions. We are where we are today because of our actions or inactions yesterday. We have either dug a hole for ourselves or built ourselves a wall, and we are the only ones who can take ourselves out.

Our current world is full of successful men and women, black and white, religious and non-religious, and young and old people from whom we can take inspiration. Some of the successful people I know—myself included—started with nothing. Starting with God and the creation of the world must teach us something.

Guy Laliberté, founder of Cirque du Soleil; Oprah Winfrey; Starbucks founder Howard Schultz; WhatsApp founder Jan Koum; former Verizon CEO Ivan Siedenberg; Russian business tycoon and Chelsea owner Roman Abramovich; Softbank CEO Masayoshi Son; and Alibaba chairman, Jack Ma, are some of the greats, just to name a few.

These successful people grew up poor. That didn't stop any of them. Today these people have broken the chains of poverty in their lives.

*On your last day on Earth, the person you became will meet the person you could have become.*

If you know that honestly you are not close to the

person you know you can be or have not even started the journey to become successful and get closer to the person you can become, there are a few things to suggest here.

We have been blessed with everything that we need to survive and become the person we ought to be. Most of the time we need not add more things—we may need to give up on some of them and harness what we have.

These things suggested here are universal. They apply to every situation and everybody, regardless of race, colour, location, age, and sexuality. Some will be a little harder to give up easily, but surely it is not impossible to do so.

> He who has health has hope, and he who has hope has everything.
>
> —Arabian proverb

Everything you want to achieve in life starts from here. First you must take care of your health—having a healthy diet and being physically active. These healthy habits should be something you embody, not some task that needs to be done. The hardest part of health is finding a way to motivate yourself to stay healthy once the initial enthusiasm wears off. Act in small steps one step at a time. Once you are able to do the little targets you set for yourself, excitement grows and catches on when you see progress. Remember that action breeds motivation.

> You only live once, but if you do it right, once is enough.
>
> —Mae West

I suggest you set long-term goals while bearing in mind that these goals will be achieved merely from the result of short-term habits that you need to do every day.

> Our deepest fear is not that we are inadequate. Our deepest fear is that we are powerful beyond measure. It is our light, not our darkness, that most frightens us. We ask ourselves, who am I to be brilliant, gorgeous, talented, and fabulous? Actually, who are you not to be? You are a child of God. Your playing small does not serve the world. There

is nothing enlightened about shrinking so that other people won't feel insecure around you. We are all meant to shine, as children do. We were born to make manifest the glory of God that is within us. It's not just in some of us; it's in everyone. And as we let our own light shine, we unconsciously give other people permission to do the same. As we are liberated from our own fear, our presence automatically liberates others.

—Marianne Williamson

The quote above says it all. Please stop playing small. Try to take the great opportunities that present themselves to you on a daily basis. Give yourself the permission and allow your dreams to become a reality. Unleash your true potential for the world to benefit from what you can achieve.

Go for your ideas, make them a reality, don't be afraid to fail, and certainly don't be afraid to succeed.

Ninety-nine percent of the failures come from people who have the habit of making excuses.

—George Washington Carver

I suggest that you accept that you are responsible for your life, no matter your starting point, weakness, and past mistakes.

Everyone else is busy with their own lives. No one will live your life for you. Own your life. When you do, that becomes the only way you can become successful, for excuses limit and prevent us from growing personally and professionally.

There is no substitute for hard work. There is no such thing as an overnight success or easy money.

—Henry Sy

Overnight success is a myth. Know that making continual small improvements every day will be added on over time and give you a desirable result. That is why you should plan but also focus on the day that is ahead of you and improve just a little every day.

> You are the average of the five people you spend the most time with.
>
> —Jim Rohn

The people we spend the most time with add up to who we become. There are associates who are less accomplished in their personal and professional lives, and there are family and friends who are more accomplished than we are. If you spend time with those who are behind you, your average will go down, and with it, your success. But if you spend time with people who are more accomplished than you, no matter how challenging that might be, you will become more successful. Look around you and see if you need to make any changes.

> Remember always that you have not only the right to be an individual; you have an

obligation to be one. You cannot make any useful contribution in life unless you do this.

—Eleanor Roosevelt

Please stop thinking about ways to make all people like you. It will not happen. That is called life. Imagine yourself as a niche market. Many people will like what you do, and there will be individuals who will not be interested in what you do. Some will even hate what you do. And no matter what you do, you will not be able to make everybody like you. This is entirely natural. Even God and Jesus Christ have haters. There is no need to justify yourself.

Remain authentic, improve, and do what you can do best every day, letting it be a consolation to you that the growing number of 'haters' means that you are doing important things.

Last but obviously not least, watch the time you spend on the Web browsing and watching television. These two are diseases of our society today. Use them wisely to improve upon your dreams.

You were designed for accomplishment, engineered for success, and endowed with seeds of greatness.

—Zig Ziglar

# CHAPTER 6

# YOU HAVE WHAT IT TAKES

A journey of a thousand miles begins with a
single step.

—Lao Tzu

Let me take you back to the story of the rich man in the
Bible, which I shared with you earlier (Matthew 25:14–
29). The Bible account says that when the rich man had
given out the talents, gold, or gifts to his servants, he went
away to a far country. Whatever you want to call what
was given to the servants, call it resources to work with.

Let us do some rough calculations to estimate how much in resources were given to the three servants in today's money value. As a unit of currency, a talent was worth about 6,000 denarii. A denarius was the usual payment for a day's labour. The most widely used currency of the day was silver, so we will use that to help us calculate the value of what the servants received.

In other words, one talent equalled sixteen years and over four months of work wage in those days. In today's money, how much money are we looking at now as far as what the rich man gave to his servants?

The Office for National Statistics has released its provisional update of the UK average salary in 2019, showing that the average full-time salary is £36,611 and the average part-time salary is £12,495 (www.findcourses.co.uk, visited on 1 October 2019).

Taking that £36,611 and multiplying it by sixteen years and five months, we discover that a talent of money in today's economy is about £601,030. The first servant received five talents. That would be about £601,030 multiplied by five, thus over £3 million. The second servant received two talents, making his total £1.2 million. The third servant received only one talent. And by 'only', I mean only £601,030.

This is no small sum of money. This is a huge responsibility. What would you do if you were this third servant and were told to responsibly manage £601,030, or even were the first servant, who was given £3million to responsibly manage, or the second servant, who was given £1.2million to responsibly manage?

*God will never give me that much, so I don't have to worry about it.* That is what you may be thinking, right?

That may be true, but it may also not be true. What God has given you in terms of resources may be worth more than these stated amounts. The talents, gifts, visions, dreams, ideas, or inspirations or whatever you call it that God has deposited in you and only you may be worth more than what we can imagine. You do have *something* that is worth thousands and millions. These things—the gifts, talents, knowledge, ideas, and resources—do not belong to you but were given to you by God for you to manage responsibly. You are His steward. How are you using the things He has given to you? Where is your money going? How are you investing it to accomplish the greatest spiritual good for the greatest number of people? How are you investing in the kingdom of God?

All of us have been given money, possessions, and positions that God wants us to use while we wait for the return of our Lord Jesus Christ. How are you using your time to invest and multiply these things—not for your own selfish gain but multiplying them for the kingdom of God and humanity as a whole?

This story of the talents also means that we are all unbelievably rich. We are all billionaires in the making. For example, when God wanted to create the furniture that we use daily in our workplace and homes for relaxation and comfort, He placed them in the trees. There is something great in you, placed in you by God, which needs to be manifested fully for the betterment of humanity.

When we believe in Jesus for eternal life, we hit the spiritual jackpot. Numerous passages in the Bible reveal this, but none better than the first three chapters of Ephesians. Ephesians reveals how rich and wealthy we are as children of God. In fact, we are rich beyond our wildest imagination.

Therefore, let me ask you again what your talents, your riches, and gifts and abilities are. Do you even know? If you do not know what they are, that is your first responsibility. How can you use them if you don't know what they are? And if you do know what gifts you have been given, how are you using them to further God's kingdom? We see in Matthew 25, verses 16–18 (KJV), how these three servants used the talents they had been given: 'Then he that had received the five talents went and traded with the same, and made them other five talents. And likewise he that had received two, he also gained other two. But he that had received one went and digged in the earth, and hid his lord's money.'

The first servant, who had been given five talents,

traded with them and doubled it to ten talents. The second servant also doubled his money. The third servant, however, the one with the least amount of money, buried it in the ground.

I am not sure what talents God has given you. I don't know what ideas, visions, or work God has assigned to you to manage responsibly. But there is one thing that I know well: your assignments in life are not insignificant. Even if it is only one talent, that is still £601,030, which can be turned into $1.5 million or even £3 million or more.

When it comes to investing your time and money in the divine assignment, there is no limit to what you can do. We must be about our master's business because the day is coming when He will return. In our parable, that day comes in Matthew 25:19, many, many years later.

Now, he who had received the five talents *immediately* went to work with his talent so was the one who received the two talents.

Life can be frustrating. Oftentimes we know what our problems are. We may even know what to do about them. But we fear that taking action is too risky, that we don't have the experience or that it's not how we pictured it or because it's too expensive, because it's too soon, because we think something better might come along, because it might not work. And you know what happens as a result? Nothing. We do nothing.

—Ryan Holiday

You and I know that you have at least one talent or even many. Why are you not manifesting fully in these ideas, talents, and visions? You have such an amazing idea and are excited about it; it makes you happy, energized, and inspired. Please do not wait until that tiny voice of *doubt* whispers to you, that voice in your head that makes you doubt your abilities, that you are not good enough, not smart enough like that person, that you are not resourced enough. Don't believe you have no network hence you just give up. That small voice that whispers lies about your life can destroy inspiration faster than anything can. One minute you know this idea is fantastic, yet just a few minutes later, you start listing all the reasons it cannot work.

The first two servants immediately went to work with what was given to them, and the passage said they doubled their investment when the master returned for accountability.

The law of diminishing intent is a principle that Jim Rohn coined and taught. John Maxwell expanded on it later. The law of diminishing intent states that with each passing moment, the intent to do something (if not already begun) diminishes rapidly. So much so that an exuberant 100 per cent intent on Wednesday afternoon can (if not acted upon immediately) dwindle to a mere 1 to 2 per cent by as early as Friday morning (less than two days later). Everyone struggles with the law of diminishing intent, at least to a degree. No exceptions.

Here is John Maxwell's explanation in an excerpt from his book:

> When I was a kid, one of my father's favourite riddles to us went like this: Five frogs are sitting on a log. Four decide to jump off. How many are left?
>
> The first time he asked me, I answered, 'One.'
>
> 'No,' he responded, 'five. Why? Because there's a difference between deciding and doing!'
>
> That was a point that Dad often drove home with us.
>
> American politician Frank Clark said, 'What great accomplishments we'd have in the world if everybody had done what they intended to do.'

*The longer you wait to act, the less likely you are to act.* This means doing something when you get clarity about an idea, a vision, or an inspiration. When your ideas are powerful and emotions are hot, that is when you have the most energy to act. Thus, whatever it is, you should act as quickly as possible. Immediately if possible. Why? Because over time, your intention and motivation for acting will diminish.

Appreciate also that when the master travelled, he did not tell them when he would return. The servants all knew that one day they would have to give an account of what has been entrusted into their care to manage, but they were not sure exactly when that time would be.

After a long time, the master returned to settle accounts with them. The talents that they had been given were not gifts after all. They were loans, if you like. The lord expected his servants to take what he had given them and use it to gain more.

I am tempted to believe that for some of us, the problem is that although we know of the riches, the ideas, and the talents and visions that have been given us, we see these special privileges as gifts rather than loans. We must also understand why God gives such gifts.

God gives these talents, visions, and knowledge to us out of love for us. God knows that if we love Him in return, we will want to give Him something in return. Remember that I said earlier on that we as humans are partnering in the creation, work, and care of this beautiful world.

God has given us some huge gifts. Why? God wants to see what we will do with them. God wants to see how much we love Him. But more than that, God wants to see if we are responsible. If we are responsible in little things, like one talent or £601,030 or the vast spiritual riches God has made available to us, then when God returns or we get to heaven, God will give us responsibility over even greater things.

The first and second servants had different abilities and responsibilities. Notwithstanding, when each had taken what he had and worked as hard as he could, they both doubled what they had been given.

And they both received the same reward. They received the same commendation. The same promotion. The same invitation. They had both doubled their master's money and therefore received the approval of the Lord and the added responsibilities in his kingdom.

Now let us look at the third servant. This man was afraid of losing what he had been given, so he buried it. He hid it in the ground so that when the master returned, he could return the one talent that was given to him.

Remember that the one talent is equivalent to today's monetary value of £601,030, and that was what the servant buried in the ground. How true is it that often it is not the people who have many abilities and talents who are afraid of using them? It is rather the people who think they do not have very many abilities and talents that usually bury their 'few' in the ground. The excuse has always been lacking resources so they sit on the sidelines and do nothing.

Maybe this is because of a fear of failure. I understand this fear of failure. We all fear stepping out onto limelight and trying something great for God. We are afraid we might fail. Remember again that I said we are partners with God in the creation, maintaining, and caring for this beautifully created world. Our fear therefore must be the idea that we are disappointing God with our sitting on the fence. And the only way we disappoint Him is by not trying to do anything with what He has given us. It's more than the fear of failure.

His lord answered and said unto him, 'Thou wicked and slothful servant, thou knewest that I reap where I sowed not, and gather where I have not strawed: Thou oughtest therefore to have put my money to the exchangers, and then at my coming I should have received mine own with usury (Matthew 25:26–27 KJV).

God wants us just to do something. The only thing God does not approve of and dislikes is for us to sit on, bury, or not manifest the talents He has given us and do nothing with them.

Gaining interest in a bank is one of the slowest ways to gain profit from money. But it is also one of the safest. And Jesus says you can do this. Do something safe with what God has given to you. Just do not sit on the talent/ money, the ideas, the call, the vision, that resource, that knowledge. If this servant had at least invested it, he would not have heard this deadly rebuke and recommendations.

Find someone or a company that is doing the sort of work or is close to the sort of vision that you get you excited about. Then go talk to the person or that organization about what you are dreaming about and learn how your dreams can change the world for the better.

Tell them you want to get started and involved, that you want to help. Ask what you can do. Ask them if you can start something small to try out first, and as you prove yourself trustworthy in that, they may give you something bigger and bigger.

By this, you are not taking a risk in stepping into the unknown. If anything, it is the person or the organization that is taking the risk, and you are just testing the waters, helping with your time and abilities. My advice is that when such an opportunity comes, grab it graciously and do not disappoint them. If they give you something small to do, do it to the best of your ability.

The safest thing you can do is to learn the trade from scratch. If you want to be the top hairstylist the world has ever known, please start from somewhere. Go to college or find a salon and begin work as a cleaner. Then you can move on to making sandwiches and coffee. Then perhaps taking hair appointments and keeping salon clients records. Then you may end up washing hair and eventually becoming an amazing hairstylist. These are all investments with the banker. Learn to serve in small ways. You will gain some confidence and will be able to begin a start-up of your own, with others possibly investing with you.

> Failure is a bend in the road, not the end of the road. Learn from failure and keep moving forward.
>
> —Roy T. Bennett

You should and must be at least willing to do the little things. But do not be like the third servant, who was not even willing to do that little investment with the banks, hence when the master returned, the servant was reproved. Rather than being promoted, the servant was demoted. Even what the third servant had was taken away from him.

# CHAPTER 7

# FINAL WORDS

I want to inspire you to keep believing in your dreams. Please understand deep down within you that things will turn out all right for you, no matter what the situation might be. Faith is an important part of life, whether you acknowledge it or not. Without faith, life would cease to have meaning. We would not be able to move from one moment to the next without doubting everything that we did.

Your success and manifesting yourself journey can and will be tough at times. When those moments finally come and get remarkably difficult, let your faith keep you going. Always say to yourself that it will get better. This affirmation will give the needed strength in times of weakness and shine light on the pathway in times of darkness. The reason having faith is so important is that it powerfully convinces you that everything will go according to plan. That's why we are nothing without faith.

Fight for your dreams and encourage yourself through faith.

# ABOUT THE AUTHOR

Jacob Opoku can usually be found reading a book, and that book will more likely be a relationship and financial book. Writing a non-fiction book about self-manifestation was always on his bucket list, and eventually, with *How and Where to Invest Your Talent*, it has become a reality. When not absorbed in the latest gripping page-turner, Jacob Opoku is filming and editing, cooking poorly, enjoying DIY projects around the house, and otherwise spending far too much time at the computer. Jacob Opoku currently lives in England with his wife and three adorable children.

He is currently working on his next book, *Before You Say 'I do'*, a must-read for all who are about to take the marriage journey and for those who are already married.